Robyn Martin's
simply delicious recipes for
crockpots &
slow cookers

Robyn Martin's
simply delicious recipes for
crockpots &
slow cookers

photographer James Ensing-Trussell

Chanel & Stylus

Thanks to Briscoes Blenheim for providing crockery and some accessories
for the photography in this book.

First published in 2009 by
Stylus Publishing Ltd and Chanel Publishers Ltd
P.O. Box 403, Whangaparaoa, New Zealand
Reprinted 2010

Distributed in Australia by
Book Group Australia
Unit 4 / 29–33 Bourke Road
Alexandria NSW 2015
Ph: (02) 9699 7220 Fax: (02) 9699 7229
www.bookgroupaustralia.com.au

Text: Robyn Martin
Photography: James Ensing-Trussell, Topic Photography
Author photograph on back cover: Syd Mannian
Publishers: Barbara Nielsen and Cliff Josephs
Editorial team: Brian O'Flaherty, Renée Lang and Diane Lowther
Design and layout: Lesley Coomer

Printed in China through Bookbuilders

ISBN 978-0-9582729-9-5

contents

introduction

The popularity of cooking in a slow cooker never ceases to amaze me. Few weeks go by where there is not someone who tells me how much they use my first slow cooker book and enjoy using this versatile small appliance. It is with their encouragement and enthusiasm for slow cooking that I have written this book with new ideas evolved from my experiments with my slow cooker.

I have certainly put mine to the test over the years and have said before that I would give my slow cooker the status of domestic god. The more I cook with it, the more I realise how many things this appliance can cook so well, and all for the energy use of an electric light bulb.

A clever piece of American marketing in the seventies introduced the world to 'Crock-pots'. This was in fact a brand name for a slow cooker. It soon became every marketer's dream — a generic name for all slow cookers. There are now many different brands, sizes and shapes of slow cookers available and more than 80 million in use today. In this book, we refer to all these appliances as slow cookers.

The slow cooker's versatility goes far beyond the food it can cook. This is one appliance that serves people across a broad age and lifestyle spectrum. It's the appliance I think every new mum should have, enabling them to put at least part of the meal on to cook before the sometimes topsy-turvy end of the day when babies often won't settle and mums are stretched to the limit of exhaustion and exasperation.

As kids grow up and the demands of after-school activities increase, a slow cooker can relieve the pressure when you walk in the door late and have a hungry family to feed.

And for those of us who work in paid or unpaid work and still love to serve home-cooked food, with a small amount of effort either the night before or in the morning before you set off, the slow cooker makes coming home after a hard day even more pleasurable.

I use mine when entertaining, for school trips where you end up cooking as parent help for a sports team and always packed it when I took my kids to the ski club. At least part of the meal was ready when we arrived back tired and hungry.

I had wanted to broadcast the benefits of slow cookers ages ago but was constrained for various reasons. I am making up for it now that I have freedom to write about things I know are important to people with real lives. You will see in this book just how delicious and attractive food cooked in the slow cooker can be.

In the pages that follow, I share the successes of many experiments with food cooked in the slow cooker. Use my discoveries to enhance your slow-cooker repertoire and develop your own dishes.

All recipes have been tested in a 4-litre Sunbeam 215–230 watt Slow Cooker
Standard metric measuring cups have been used.
1 cup — 250ml
1 teaspoon — 5ml
1 tablespoon — 15ml

the basics

*and amazing things you can make
in your slow cooker*

*Understand what your slow cooker
can do and you will get so much more from this
versatile small appliance.*

- Preheating the slow cooker is not necessary for successful slow cooking. If you remember, you can preheat, but as speed is not the focus of this cooking method there is no need to do this. If you are in a hurry and want to speed up cooking time, the cooker can be preheated, and hot or boiling liquids will help too.

- Slow cooking makes an excellent job of drawing fat from food which, if left to go cold, will settle on top and solidify for easy removal. If you are serving the food when it is hot, use a fat sucker, paper towels or try pouring the layer of fat from the food before serving.

- The slow cooker can be used very successfully for pot roasting. A whole piece of meat is browned first, then cooked by moist heat in the slow cooker.

- Add salt at the end of cooking if possible as salt draws moisture from food, which makes it less succulent.

- Most slow-cooker recipes that are cooked on LOW can be cooked on HIGH for half the specified LOW cooking time.

- Slow cooking uses moist heat from steam or cooking liquid to cook, so anything that cooks well with liquid or steam will probably cook well in the slow cooker. It will not roast as this requires dry heat to brown the meat during cooking.

- Every time you lift the lid on your slow cooker, you lose heat, so resist the temptation to do this too often. I find it is best to try to stir many recipes halfway through cooking to make sure meat in particular does not dry out during the slow-cooking process. If you have a chance to do this take it, but if you don't, there is no need to fret.

- To ensure food is always safe to eat, never cool food in the slow cooker. Transfer it to another dish, cool quickly and refrigerate. Reheat thoroughly before serving.

- The inside edge of the slow cooker bowl heats any food in contact with it. This food will cook more quickly and, if no moisture is present, will brown. For this reason bread cooked in the slow cooker browns on the base and sides, and vegetables such as kumara and potatoes cook better if put on the bottom of the slow-cooker bowl.

- Most foods release water during slow cooking which does not evaporate as it would in conventional cooking. When adapting recipes to slow cook, reduce the cooking liquid by half. If necessary, add extra hot liquid towards the end of cooking.

- I have had great success cooking dried beans in the slow cooker, getting them started with boiling water. Low-wattage slow cookers may not be as successful as the Sunbeam Slow Cooker these recipes were tested in. Check the wattage of your cooker. For success, I would recommend a cooker of at least 215–230 watts.

- Casserole-style food cooked in the slow cooker can be thickened at the end of cooking if wished by mixing flour or cornflour to a smooth paste with water, then mixing into the slow cooker. Turn the cooker to HIGH and cook, covered, for 10–15 minutes or until thickened.

- I cannot see the point of browning onions or meat when slow cooking because most people using this cooking method lack time — and who needs anything extra to do? If you are cooking food on HIGH for half the LOW cooking time, place the chopped onions on the bottom of the slow cooker bowl to make sure they are well cooked when you are ready to serve.

divine pesto bread

I am still in awe at how well bread cooks in the slow cooker. Use this idea for your own special bread.

1 sachet instant dried yeast
1 tablespoon sugar
2 cups warm water
$1/4$ teaspoon salt
4–5 cups flour suitable for bread making
$1/2$ cup basil pesto
$1^1/2$ cups grated tasty cheese

Place yeast, sugar, water and salt in a large bowl. Mix in enough flour to make a stiff dough. Turn onto a floured board and work in more flour to make a stiff dough that can be kneaded. Knead dough until smooth and elastic. The dough will spring back when poked with your finger when it has been kneaded enough. Roll dough out to a 72 x 22cm rectangle. Spread pesto over dough and sprinkle with cheese. Roll dough up from the long side and curl into a well-oiled slow cooker. Cover and cook on HIGH for $2^1/2$ hours.

The bread is cooked if it sounds hollow when tapped. It will look pale on top but when turned out it will be brown on the sides that touch the slow cooker bowl. Turn onto a cooling rack. Serve warm if wished.

to freshen stale bread or bread rolls

Wet bread or rolls under cold tap. Place in the slow cooker. Cover and heat on HIGH for 30 minutes.

crocked garlic bread

1 round cob loaf about
17cm in diameter
6 cloves garlic
100g butter

Cut bread into segments almost to centre. Crush, peel and finely chop garlic. Soften butter and mix in garlic until combined. Use to spread between each segment of bread. Place bread in the slow cooker. Cover with a paper towel and heat on HIGH for 30 minutes.
Serve hot.

to cook a whole chicken

This is a very basic way to cook a chicken to use as is or in another dish. For my money, the flavour of the chicken seems to be much nicer than those cooked conventionally.

1 medium chicken
1 lemon
fresh herbs

Wash chicken cavity and dry with paper towels. Cut lemon in half and place in chicken cavity with herbs. Place in the slow cooker. Cover and cook on LOW for 8 hours. Use as wished.

Serves 4—6

ski club mulled wine

Just about every ski club in the country serves mulled wine at some time in the season. Here is a great way to keep your mulled wine warm for enjoyment over a cold evening après ski.

2 bottles red wine
$1/4$ cup sugar
12 whole cloves
2 cinnamon sticks
1 orange

Pour wine into the slow cooker. Add sugar, cloves and cinnamon sticks. Slice orange and add to the slow cooker. Cover and heat on HIGH for 1 hour. To keep hot turn to LOW.

Makes 1.5 litres

dry-roasted garlic

A bulb of garlic is made up of many cloves.

1 bulb garlic

Place garlic in a small metal pie dish. Pour $1/2$ cup of water into the slow cooker. Sit garlic dish in this. Cover and cook on HIGH for 2 hours.
Serve as an accompaniment to other dishes or squeeze garlic out of skins and use in a vegetable mash.

grapefruit marmalade

Cooking the fruit pulp in a slow cooker draws out the pectin required for a good set for this marmalade. Higher temperatures than can be obtained in a slow cooker are required to make any marmalade or jam, so the slow cooker is best used to get better flavour and setting from preserves that require overnight soaking of the fruit.

4 large grapefruit
2 good-tasting lemons
6 cups water
sugar

Wash grapefruit and lemons and cut in half. Squeeze juice from fruit and reserve the pips. Finely shred skin from 3 grapefruit and 3 lemon halves and place in a muslin bag. Roughly chop remaining skins and place in the slow cooker with juice, pips and water. Add shredded skins in muslin bag. Cover and cook on HIGH for 4 hours.

Pour the slow cooker contents through a sieve into a measuring jug. Calculate the amount of sugar required, allowing 1 cup of sugar for each cup of juice. Pour juice into a large saucepan or preserving pan. Add contents of muslin bag and sugar. Stir over a medium heat until sugar has dissolved. Bring to the boil and boil rapidly for about 20 minutes or until setting test is reached. This is when a small amount of marmalade is put on a chilled saucer, left to cool for a couple of minutes then forms a channel that stays apart after your finger is dragged through the middle. Take marmalade off heat while checking for setting.

Pour into hot, clean, dry jars. Seal when cold.

Makes about 7 cups

soups

Hearty soups of substance that are a meal in themselves or a lighter style, flavour-packed 'potage' to start a meal are easily cooked in the slow cooker for enjoyment at any time of the year.

hot-sour thai squid soup

500g cut fresh or frozen
squid rings
1 onion
2 cloves garlic
2 kaffir lime leaves
2 limes
4 thin slices root ginger
4 cups fish or vegetable stock
1/2 teaspoon prepared
minced chilli
2 tablespoons fresh lime juice
2 tablespoons Thai fish sauce
2 teaspoons palm or brown sugar
1/4 cup chopped fresh coriander
kaffir lime leaves

Thaw squid if using frozen. Place prepared squid in the slow cooker. Peel onion and chop finely. Crush, peel and finely chop garlic. Finely shred kaffir lime leaves. Cut limes in half, squeeze juice over squid and place halves in the slow cooker with onion, garlic, lime leaves, root ginger and vegetable stock. Cover and cook on LOW for 2 hours.

Just before serving, mix in chilli, lime juice, fish sauce, sugar and coriander. Check seasoning, adding more lime juice, sugar and/or chilli so soup has a hot-sour flavour. Serve garnished with a kaffir lime leaf.

Serves 4

parsnip and thyme soup

Reduce the liquid and serve this as a vegetable purée if wished. Either way, it is truly scrumptious.

6 parsnips
1 onion
2 cloves garlic
4 sprigs fresh thyme
1 bay leaf
3 cups chicken stock
1 cup milk
ground nutmeg
fresh thyme

Peel parsnips, trim ends and cut into 2cm pieces. Place in the slow cooker. Peel onion and chop finely. Crush, peel and finely chop garlic. Place onion, garlic, sprigs of thyme, bay leaf and chicken stock in the slow cooker. Cover and cook on HIGH for 6 hours.

Mix in milk and cook for a further hour. Purée the mixture in a blender, food processor or with a food wand. Serve hot, garnished with grated nutmeg and fresh thyme.

Serves 3—4

summer vegetable soup with pistou

This is a specialty of Provence and is made with ceremony each year once the garlic is harvested. Traditionally, garlic is planted on the shortest day and harvested on the longest day. The soup is made from fresh garden vegetables and is topped with the pistou, a mixture of fresh basil, garlic, olive oil and Parmesan or pecorino cheese. This soup cannot be cooked on LOW unless you soak the beans before cooking.

1 cup cannellini or haricot beans

2 medium potatoes

2 carrots

2 onions

2 courgettes

3 tomatoes

1 bouquet garni made by tying parsley, thyme, bay leaf and a celery top together

6 cups boiling water

1 cup small macaroni

salt and pepper

Place beans in the slow cooker. Peel potatoes and carrots and cut into 1cm cubes. Place on top of beans. Peel onions, slice thinly and place on top of carrots. Trim courgettes, cut into quarters lengthwise and cut into thirds. Arrange on top of onions. Chop tomatoes roughly and place on courgettes. Add bouquet garni. Pour boiling water over. Cover and cook on HIGH for 8–10 hours.

Twenty minutes before serving, mix in macaroni. Cover and cook for 20 minutes. Season to taste with salt and pepper. Serve topped with pistou and accompanied with crusty bread.

Serves 4–6

PISTOU

6 cloves garlic

1/2 teaspoon salt

1 cup firmly packed fresh basil leaves

1/2 cup finely grated Parmesan or pecorino cheese

1/2 cup olive oil

PISTOU

Crush and peel garlic. Place garlic, salt and basil in a small food processor or mortar bowl and process or grind to a paste. Add cheese and oil, a little at a time, processing or grinding with a pestle until a thick paste forms.

mexican corn, chicken and tomato soup with cheesy tortillas

2 onions
2 cloves garlic
4 chicken drumsticks
500g bag frozen whole kernel corn
2 cans Mexican flavoured tomatoes
4 cups chicken stock
2 corn tortillas
1 cup grated tasty cheese
celery leaves

Peel onions and chop finely. Crush, peel and finely chop garlic. Remove skin from chicken and discard. Place onion, garlic, chicken, corn, tomatoes and chicken stock in the slow cooker. Cover and cook on HIGH for 6–8 hours.

Remove chicken from bones and return chicken meat to the slow cooker. Grill one side of the tortillas until lightly golden. Turn over and top with grated cheese. Grill until cheese is golden. Cut into wedges or shards and serve with the soup.

Serves 6

tip

If you are not using all this soup when it is cooked, transfer it to another bowl and cool it quickly before refrigerating.

bacon and bean soup

This is a thick soup and can be thinned with boiling water before serving if wished.

2 onions
3 cloves garlic
1 leek
1 cup white beans
1 cup orange lentils
1 bacon hock
5 cups boiling chicken stock
2 large handfuls baby spinach
salt and pepper
shaved Parmesan cheese

Peel onions and chop finely. Crush, peel and finely chop garlic. Trim leek and cut halfway through the middle lengthwise. Wash leek thoroughly, then cut into 1cm slices. Place the onion, garlic, leek, beans, lentils, bacon hock and chicken stock in the slow cooker. Cover and cook on HIGH for 8–10 hours.

Remove hock from the slow cooker. Peel off rind and discard. The meat will fall from the bone. Cut meat into chunks. Return to the slow cooker. Mix in spinach leaves. Season with salt and pepper.

Serve hot garnished with Parmesan shavings.

Serves 4

beetroot soup

Beetroot is the new wonder vegetable, rich in antioxidants and a great cleanser for the body. Don't think you have a terrible disease when it passes out next day. The horseradish used in this recipe is ready made.

2 onions
3 cloves garlic
4 fresh beetroot
1 apple
2 tablespoons cider vinegar
1 tablespoon traditional German horseradish
2 cups water
salt and pepper
sour cream

Peel onions and chop finely. Crush, peel and finely chop garlic. Trim ends from beetroot. Peel beetroot and cut into 1cm cubes. Peel and core apple. Cut into eighths. Place onions, garlic, beetroot, apple, vinegar, horseradish and water in the slow cooker. Cover and cook on LOW for 8 hours.

Purée in a blender, food processor or with a food wand. Season with salt and pepper. Serve hot, garnished with sour cream.

Serves 2–3

french fish soup

Fish is not something I would usually cook in a slow cooker, as most fish is best cooked for a short time. A fish soup is different, still respecting that most fish and shellfish are best cooked for short rather than long times. This soup was one of my flavour delights when testing recipes for this book.

2 fish heads or 2 small whole, cleaned fish such as butterfish
2 onions
3 cloves garlic
3 stalks celery
1 carrot
2 leeks, white part only
1 branch fennel
1 bouquet garni made by tying a sprig of parsley, thyme and a bay leaf together
400g can diced tomatoes
1 cup dry white wine, e.g. sauvignon blanc
2 cups water
salt and pepper

TO SERVE
1 medium fillet monkfish
8 fresh mussels
8 prawns
1/2 cup aïoli
pinch saffron
croutons

Chop fish heads in half, or leave fish whole and place in the slow cooker. Peel onions and chop finely. Crush, peel and finely chop garlic. Wash celery and chop stalks into thirds. Peel carrot and cut into 1cm cubes. Trim leeks, slit down the middle lengthwise and wash thoroughly. Cut leeks into 1cm slices. Place onions, garlic, celery, carrot, leeks, fennel, bouquet garni, tomatoes, wine and water in the slow cooker. Cover and cook on HIGH for 6 hours.

Remove fish heads, bouquet garni and fennel and discard. Cut monkfish into 2cm cubes. Scrub mussels and remove beards. Add monkfish, mussels and prawns to the slow cooker. Cover and cook for a further 15 minutes. Discard any mussels that do not open. Mix saffron into aïoli. Serve soup accompanied by saffron aïoli and croutons.

Serves 4

malaysian oxtail or beef shin soup

Oxtails are something to be savoured but, sadly, they are not always available. If you cannot find one or they are too pricey, use beef shin instead.

1 oxtail or 500g beef shin on the bone
2 onions
2 potatoes
1 large kumara
2 teaspoons cumin seeds
2 star anise
2 teaspoons coriander seeds
1 cinnamon stick
6 cups beef stock
salt and pepper
chopped parsley
crusty bread

Have the butcher cut the oxtail into pieces or use a cleaver to do this yourself. Place oxtail or beef shin in the slow cooker. Peel onions and chop coarsely. Peel potatoes and kumara and cut into 2cm cubes. Wrap cumin seeds, star anise and coriander seeds in a piece of muslin or clean cloth and tie to hold the spices. Place the onions, potatoes, kumara, tied spices, cinnamon stick and stock in the slow cooker. Cover and cook on HIGH for 8–10 hours.

Remove bones and spices. Season with salt and pepper. Serve soup garnished with chopped parsley and crusty bread.

Serves 4–6

tip

Whole spices withstand being cooked in the slow cooker better than ground spices and are now readily available in the spice section of most supermarkets.

hannah's indian pumpkin soup

My daughter Hannah has found the slow cooker I gave her fantastic for soups. This is her favourite.

2 onions
2 cloves garlic
750g peeled and deseeded pumpkin
425g can coconut milk
2 teaspoons curry powder
1 teaspoon ground cumin
$1/2$ teaspoon mixed spice
4 cups chicken stock
chopped fresh coriander

Peel onions and chop finely. Crush, peel and finely chop garlic. Cut pumpkin into 2cm cubes. Place onions, garlic, pumpkin, coconut milk, curry powder, cumin, mixed spice and stock into the slow cooker. Cover and cook on HIGH for 4–6 hours.

Mash pumpkin with a potato masher or purée in a blender or food processor. Serve garnished with chopped fresh coriander.

Serves 4

golden glow pumpkin soup

Make sure you read the ingredient listing if using vegetable stock powder. Some brands contain MSG (monosodium glutamate flavour enhancer, E number 621). Anything that requires the addition of artificial flavour enhancer has no place on the table of any self-respecting cook!

1 onion	Peel onion and chop finely. Crush, peel and finely chop garlic. Peel kumara
2 cloves garlic	and cut kumara and pumpkin into 2cm cubes. Peel carrot, trim ends and
1 golden kumara	cut into 1cm pieces. Place onion, garlic, kumara, pumpkin, carrots, split peas
500g peeled pumpkin	and stock into the slow cooker. Cover and cook on HIGH for 6—8 hours.
2 carrots	Mash with a potato masher and season with salt and pepper. Cook bacon
1 cup yellow split peas	until crisp. Serve soup hot, garnished with crispy bacon and sundried tomato
5 cups cold vegetable stock	pesto.
4 rashers bacon	
sundried tomato pesto	Serves 4—6

chicken

Where would we be without wonderful chicken to provide the base for so many delicious dishes we can slow cook? Chicken combines so well with so many flavours, and the ability of its different cuts to be substituted one for the other gives any chicken recipe supreme versatility.

john's lemon and thyme chicken

1 medium chicken
1 good-tasting lemon
4 cloves garlic
6 fresh thyme sprigs or
1 tablespoon dried thyme

Using your fingers, gently separate chicken skin from the flesh of the chicken to make a pocket. Run your fingers between skin on legs as well. Cut lemon into thin slices. Crush, peel and cut garlic into thin slivers. Place lemon slices, garlic and thyme under loosened chicken skin. Place chicken in the slow cooker. Cover and cook on LOW for 6—8 hours. Liquid will come from the chicken during cooking.

Remove from the slow cooker and cut into portions to serve.

Serves 4—6

tuscan cellar chicken

10 chicken drumsticks
1 onion
2 cloves garlic
3 stalks celery
1 sprig rosemary
2 bay leaves
$1/4$ cup balsamic vinegar
$1/2$ cup chicken stock
2 tablespoons cornflour
2 tablespoons water
fresh herbs

Cut knobbly end from drumsticks. Remove skin from chicken and discard. Peel onion and chop finely. Crush, peel and finely chop garlic. Trim celery and cut into 1cm pieces. Place rosemary and bay leaves in the slow cooker. Top with chicken, onion and garlic. Pour balsamic vinegar and stock over. Cover and cook on LOW for 8—10 hours.

Half an hour before serving, mix cornflour and water together and stir into chicken mixture. Cover and cook for 30 minutes. Serve garnished with fresh herbs.

Serves 4—6

busy busy chicken

If I saw a recipe with a name like this I would immediately consider it was a must for my busy, busy life. This is definitely a recipe for those with little time but who love to prepare and enjoy food with great flavours. Use any noodle variety for this recipe.

1 medium chicken
4 cloves garlic
3 teaspoons ground cumin
2 tablespoons paprika
1 teaspoon prepared minced chilli
$\frac{1}{2}$ cup hot chicken stock
1 onion
2 whole cloves
2 bay leaves
1 bunch spinach
2 bundles egg noodles
fresh herbs or spring onion greens for garnish

If you have time, remove as much skin as you can from chicken. Place chicken in the slow cooker. Crush, peel and mash garlic. Mix garlic, cumin, paprika, chilli and stock together. Pour over chicken. Peel onion and press cloves into onion flesh. Add onion and bay leaves to the slow cooker, pressing into liquid. Cover and cook on LOW for 8–10 hours.

Ten minutes before serving, remove chicken from the slow cooker and add washed spinach leaves to the slow cooker. Cover and cook for 10 minutes. When ready to serve, cook noodles to packet directions. Drain. Cut chicken into serving-sized pieces. Divide noodles among 6 bowls. Place a serving-sized portion of chicken over noodles. Spoon cooking liquid and spinach over. Garnish with fresh herbs or spring onion greens.

Serves 6

tip

Spinach is a vegetable with a lot of water in it, so it cooks well when left to 'sweat' on top of food that has been cooked in the slow cooker. Cook it with just the water clinging to its leaves from washing for only a very short cooking time.

paper-wrapped chicken

When I first experimented with this concept, I stood by with a fire extinguisher as I wasn't sure if the paper would catch fire. It didn't even scorch when I cooked these on HIGH for half the cooking time. Use this idea to trap other flavours during the slow-cooking process.

4 x 300 square cm pieces baking paper

4 skinned and boned chicken breasts

4 tablespoons grated root ginger

4 kaffir lime leaves

4 x 6cm pieces lemon grass

With the paper on a work surface, place a chicken breast in centre of each piece. Spread a tablespoon of root ginger over each breast. Top each with a kaffir lime leaf. Crush lemon grass with the back of a knife and place a piece on top of each breast. Wrap each breast tightly in paper. Arrange over base and sides of the slow cooker, not on top of one another. Cover and cook on LOW for 6 hours.

Carefully remove paper packets from the slow cooker and place on a serving plate. Cut a cross in top of each packet and peel back paper. Serve with Thai Sauce.

THAI SAUCE

¼ cup sweet chilli sauce

2 tablespoons soy sauce

1 tablespoon chopped fresh coriander

THAI SAUCE

Mix sweet chilli and soy sauces and coriander together.

Serves 4

tip

Cooking food wrapped in paper is a well-tested way to ensure food has maximum flavour and is a good option for fat-free cooking. Try growing a kaffir lime in a pot to enjoy the flavour of this delicious ingredient.

cuban chicken

Think of Cuba and cigars jump into your head, rather than delicious Cuban food. However, the Cubans have some special flavours that put a unique stamp on their cooking. Try this and see what I mean.

1 onion

4 cloves garlic

1 orange

2 limes

2 large or 4 small skinned and boned chicken breasts

1 tablespoon dried oregano

425g can diced tomatoes in juice

1 red capsicum

Peel onion and chop finely. Crush, peel and finely slice garlic. Grate rind from orange and limes, then squeeze juice. Cut chicken breasts into 2cm wide strips. Place chicken, onion, garlic, orange and lime rind and juice and oregano in the slow cooker. Pour tomatoes over. Cover and cook on LOW for 8–10 hours.

Half an hour before serving, cut capsicum in half and remove seeds. Cut flesh into 1cm cubes. Mix into the slow cooker. Cover and cook for 20–30 minutes.

Serves 4

chicken and pumpkin curry

Always taste your curry for the right flavour intensity before you serve and adjust accordingly, as some herbs and spices lose or intensify flavour when slow cooked.

300g piece peeled pumpkin
4 skinned and boned chicken thighs
2 tablespoons red curry paste
1 tablespoon fish sauce
1 teaspoon brown sugar
440g can coconut milk
2 kaffir lime leaves
kaffir lime leaves

Cut pumpkin into 2cm chunks. Place in the slow cooker. Cut chicken into 2cm pieces. Place on top of pumpkin. Mix curry paste, fish sauce, sugar and coconut milk together. Pour over chicken. Poke kaffir lime leaves into mixture. Cover and cook on LOW for 8 hours.

Serve with steamed rice, garnished with kaffir lime leaves or fresh herbs.

Serves 4

chicken delicious

2 onions

2 cloves garlic

I small eggplant

8 skinned and boned chicken thighs

$^1/_4$ cup sundried tomatoes

2 teaspoons ground ginger

I teaspoon ground cinnamon

I teaspoon ground turmeric

$^1/_2$ cup hot chicken stock

salt and pepper

$^1/_2$ cup chopped fresh coriander

2 tablespoons chopped fresh mint

Peel onions and chop finely. Crush, peel and finely chop garlic. Trim ends from eggplant. Cut eggplant into 2cm cubes. Place chicken in the slow cooker with eggplant, onion, garlic and sundried tomatoes. Mix ginger, cinnamon and turmeric into stock and pour over chicken. Cover and cook on LOW for 8 hours.

Season with salt and pepper. Mix coriander and mint together and sprinkle over chicken to serve.

Serves 4—6

harvest chicken

Vintage marks the end of a season of hard work in a vineyard so what better way to celebrate nature's bounty than a harvest lunch shared with family and friends. We invited 25 for lunch and served a conventionally cooked version of this dish, modified here for slow-cooker cooking. The flavours are delicious and make juniper berries an interesting ingredient to have in the pantry. They are also used to flavour gin! You can use red grapes in this if you prefer, but the colour of the juices makes the chicken look as though it is not cooked properly so you may need to reassure those who share your meal table.

8 skinned chicken thigh cutlets
4 rashers bacon
2 onions
3 cloves garlic
3 stalks celery
6 sprigs fresh thyme
2 bay leaves
8 juniper berries
$\frac{1}{2}$ cup chicken stock or white wine
2 cups seedless green grapes

Remove any fat from chicken and discard. Derind bacon and cut rashers in half. Wrap half a rasher around each thigh cutlet. Peel onions and chop finely. Crush, peel and finely chop garlic. Trim celery and cut into 2cm pieces. Place onion, garlic, thyme, bay leaves, juniper berries and stock or wine in the slow cooker. Add chicken thighs and sprinkle celery over. Cover and cook on LOW for 8 hours.

Half an hour before the dish is ready to serve add grapes to the slow cooker. Cover and cook for 30 minutes. Thicken if wished or serve with crusty bread to mop up the juices.

Serves 4—6

tip

If seedless grapes are not available, choose large grapes and cut them in half to remove the seeds. Seeds in this dish will spoil the eating experience.

sage, onion and apple chicken with baby potatoes

8 chicken drumsticks
2 cloves garlic
1 onion
2 rashers bacon
10 small potatoes
$^1/_4$ cup coarsely torn fresh sage leaves
1 tablespoon fresh thyme leaves
$^1/_2$ cup apple juice concentrate
salt and pepper
fresh herbs

Cut knobbly joint from drumsticks. Remove skin from chicken and discard. Crush, peel and chop garlic. Peel onion and chop finely. Derind bacon and chop rashers into small pieces. Wash potatoes and cut in half. Place potatoes cut-side down over the base of the slow cooker. Arrange chicken on top. Scatter with sage and thyme, onion, garlic and bacon. Pour apple juice over. Cover and cook on LOW for 8–10 hours.

Season with salt and pepper. Garnish with fresh herbs.

Serves 4–6

cheryl's speedy crockpot chook

Cheryl Talbot is the cousin of my dear school friend Dayl. When she told me how useful she found my first slow cooker book, I asked her for her favourite slow cooker recipe. This is what she gave me.

1 medium chicken
2 tablespoons flour
1/4 cup liquid honey
2 tablespoons soy sauce
1 tablespoon sesame seeds
salt and pepper
1/2 cup water

Wash chicken and pat dry with paper towels. Dust with flour and place in the slow cooker. Drizzle honey and soy sauce over and sprinkle with sesame seeds. Season with salt and pepper. Pour water around chicken. Cover and cook on HIGH for 4–6 hours.

Thicken juices if wished and serve in the slow cooker bowl. Alternatively, place chicken in a dish, cool and refrigerate. Pour chicken juices into a jug or bowl and refrigerate. The juices will set like a jelly and can be cut into pieces like an aspic to serve with cold chicken.

Serves 4–6

chicken with garlic

Garlic has many health benefits and when cooked does not make you smell like a walking garlic bulb. Garlic is one of my must-have ingredients so a dish that provides lots of soft, melt-in-the-mouth cooked garlic is a favourite in our home.

6 chicken pieces
2 bulbs garlic
$1/4$ cup capers
$1/4$ cup chicken stock
$1/4$ cup red wine vinegar
1 tablespoon dried thyme
salt and pepper
thyme sprigs

Remove skin from chicken pieces and discard. Place chicken in the slow cooker. Remove outer dry skin from garlic bulb and break off garlic cloves. Place on top of chicken. Sprinkle capers over. Mix stock, vinegar and thyme together and pour over chicken. Cover and cook on LOW for 8 hours.

Season with salt and pepper. Serve chicken with garlic cloves on top and cooking juices spooned over. The garlic is squeezed out of the skin to eat. Garnish with fresh thyme.

Serves 4–6

vineyard chicken

When I lived in the city, this was the sort of dish I dreamed of making. Now living on a small vineyard in Marlborough I have the opportunity to make such delicious dishes. If you don't have access to fresh vine leaves, don't worry. This will still taste excellent without them.

4–6 fresh vine leaves
12 chicken drumsticks
12 rashers bacon
1 onion
2 cloves garlic
2 tablespoons honey
½ cup verjuice or red grape juice
1 tablespoon dill seeds
salt and pepper
fresh vine leaves

Wash vine leaves thoroughly and arrange in the bottom of the slow cooker. Remove skin from chicken and discard. Chop knobbly joint from drumsticks. Derind bacon and wrap a rasher around each drumstick. Peel onion and chop finely. Crush, peel and finely chop garlic. Mix honey, verjuice and dill seeds together. Arrange chicken over grape leaves. Sprinkle with onion and garlic and pour verjuice mixture over. Cover and cook on LOW for 8 hours.

Season with salt and pepper. Serve on fresh, clean vine leaves with the juices poured over.

Serves 4–6

tip

Verjuice is made from unripened grapes used to make unfermented grape juice. It is sold in delicatessens, some supermarkets and makes appearances in some foodie gift baskets. Use grape juice if you do not have access to verjuice.

believe-it-or-not chicken and grilled cheese tortillas

One of the easiest things to do with your slow cooker is to take a chicken from its bag, place it in the slow cooker and leave it to cook while you are gone for the day. If you have no time to put any other ingredients together, this simple action can make life so much easier when you arrive home and have hungry mouths to feed. The alternatives for this cooked chicken are endless so the idea I give here is just one option.

1 medium chicken

Place chicken in the slow cooker. Cover and cook on LOW for 8–10 hours.

Remove chicken from the cooker and cut flesh from bones. Use to make tortillas, pie, sandwiches, tacos, a salad or any other dish calling for cooked chicken.

TORTILLAS
8 corn or wheat tortillas or other flat bread
baby spinach
grated carrot
avocado slices
tomato relish
1 cup grated cheese

TORTILLAS

Place tortillas on a board or clean work surface. Place spinach in a 2cm strip down one side of tortilla. Follow with grated carrot, avocado, relish and chicken. Roll tortilla up and place in an ovenproof dish. Sprinkle cheese over and grill until cheese is melted and golden.

Serves 4–6

tip

Cooking chicken this way gives it a magnificent flavour. It can be used hot or cooled quickly and served cold.

soy and ginger chicken with cucumber sesame salad

1 onion
2 cloves garlic
2 tablespoons grated root ginger
2 x 8cm pieces orange rind
$^1/_4$ cup soy sauce
1 teaspoon Chinese five spice powder
4 skinned, boned chicken breasts

Peel onion and chop finely. Crush, peel and finely chop garlic. Mix onion, garlic, ginger, orange rind, soy sauce and five spice powder together. Place chicken in the slow cooker and pour soy sauce mixture over. Cover and cook on LOW for 8 hours.

Arrange Cucumber Sesame Salad on a serving platter. Cut chicken into slices and arrange on platter. Spoon some of the cooking juices over chicken.

CUCUMBER SESAME SALAD
2 spring onions
1 telegraph cucumber
$^1/_4$ cup chopped coriander
3 tablespoons white vinegar
1 tablespoon sesame oil

CUCUMBER SESAME SALAD
Trim spring onions and slice finely. Cut cucumber into long, thin slices using a wide blade peeler. Mix spring onions, cucumber, coriander, vinegar and sesame oil together to combine.

Serves 4

tip

Any skinned and boned chicken cut can be used for this and most other chicken recipes. Buy what is on special – the best part of slow cooking is that you will not have to adjust the cooking time if you use another chicken cut.

ginger chicken breasts

4 skinned and boned chicken breasts
2 spring onions
2 tablespoons grated root ginger
1 teaspoon grated orange rind
1 tablespoon white vinegar
1/2 teaspoon sesame oil
1/4 cup sweet sherry
1/4 cup chicken stock
spring onion curls

Cut chicken breasts through centre on thin side, to 0.5cm from long edge. Open chicken breasts out and flatten. Trim spring onions and chop very finely or chop in a small food processor. Mix spring onions, ginger, orange rind, vinegar and sesame oil together until combined. Divide among chicken breasts, spreading to cover cut surface. Roll chicken up from long side or, if breasts are too thick to roll, fold breast in half. Arrange chicken in the slow cooker. Pour sherry and chicken stock over. Cover and cook on LOW for 8 hours.

Serve sliced, garnished with spring onion curls.

Serves 4–6

chicken marrakesh

1 onion
2 cloves garlic
8 chicken pieces
2 teaspoons smoked paprika
2 teaspoons ground ginger
¹/₂ cup chicken stock
1 lemon
1 large branch parsley
4 stems fresh coriander
extra fresh coriander
pita bread

Peel onion and chop finely. Crush, peel and chop garlic. Remove skin from chicken and discard. Place chicken pieces in the slow cooker. Sprinkle onion and garlic over. Mix paprika and ginger with chicken stock. Pour over chicken. Cut lemon into eighths. Add to the slow cooker with parsley and coriander stems. Cover and cook on LOW for 8–10 hours.

Serve garnished with fresh coriander and accompanied with pita bread.

Serves 4–6

chicken provençal

The secret of this dish is to have good-flavoured tomatoes. Canned varieties are the most reliable but if you have your own growing, these are bound to taste better than most supermarket varieties.

8 chicken pieces
1 onion
4 cloves garlic
425g can chopped tomatoes
2 tablespoons tomato paste
1 cup black olives
2 teaspoons dried marjoram
2 teaspoons dried basil
1 bay leaf
salt and pepper
fresh herbs

Remove skin from chicken and discard. Place chicken in the slow cooker. Peel onion and chop finely. Crush, peel and finely chop garlic. Place onion, garlic, tomatoes, tomato paste, olives, marjoram, basil and bay leaf in the slow cooker, mixing to combine ingredients. Cover and cook on LOW for 8–10 hours.

Season with salt and pepper. Serve garnished with fresh herbs.

Serves 4–6

thursday night chicken curry with the boys

We have a couple of friends who like to celebrate making it to Thursday each working week by eating at the local (and very good) Asian 'melting pot' restaurant. A curry always features in their choice of food, so here is one you can make at home, boys, when it is too miserable to venture out. There are many stores selling whole spices now, even in small centres. I buy mine at the local Bin Inn store in Blenheim.

6 chicken thighs
1 onion
3 cloves garlic
1 tablespoon grated root ginger
1 tablespoon black mustard seeds
2 tablespoons tamarind paste
2 teaspoons fenugreek seeds
2 tablespoons coriander seeds
2 teaspoons ground turmeric
425g can chopped tomatoes in juice
$1/2$ cup chicken stock
$1/2$ teaspoon prepared minced chilli
fresh herbs

Remove skin from chicken and discard. Place chicken in the slow cooker. Peel onion and chop finely. Crush, peel and finely chop garlic. Add onion, garlic, ginger, mustard seeds, tamarind, fenugreek, coriander, turmeric, tomatoes and chicken stock to slow cooker. Cover and cook on LOW for 8 hours.

Just before serving, mix in chilli. Thicken if wished. Serve garnished with fresh herbs.

Serves 4–6

tip

Tamarind paste is available from Asian provision stores and some supermarkets. You may have to look in the international section of the supermarket to find it.

italian chicken braise

8 chicken pieces
2 tablespoons flour
1 onion
2 cloves garlic
2 stalks celery
1 tablespoon dried sage
1 tablespoon dried rosemary leaves
$1/2$ cup white wine
1 teaspoon chicken stock powder or 1 stock cube
440g can chopped tomatoes
salt and pepper
fresh celery leaves

Remove skin from chicken and discard. Place flour in a plastic bag and toss chicken in it to coat. Place chicken in the slow cooker. Peel onion and chop finely. Crush, peel and finely chop garlic. Trim celery, reserving leaves. Cut stalks into 2cm pieces. Add onion, garlic, celery, sage and rosemary to the slow cooker. Mix wine and stock powder or cube together. Pour into the slow cooker with tomatoes. Mix gently to combine. Place celery leaves on top of mixture. Cover and cook on LOW for 8 hours.

Season with salt and pepper. Discard celery leaves. Serve garnished with fresh celery leaves.

Serves 4–6

tip

Removing the skin from chicken removes a good portion of the chicken fat, making the end dish a lot healthier without compromising on flavour.

cockscomb pie

Use cold for a double-crusted pie.

2 carrots
2 stalks celery
I onion
I ham steak
10 button mushrooms
I medium chicken
I cup hot chicken stock
I teaspoon dried thyme
2 sheets flaky pastry
25g butter
3 tablespoons flour
2 tablespoons chopped parsley

Peel carrots and cut into 1–2cm cubes. Trim celery and cut into 1cm slices. Peel onion and chop finely. Derind ham steak and cut into 1cm cubes. Wipe mushrooms and trim stalks if necessary. Place carrots and onion in the slow cooker. Place chicken on top of vegetables. Add celery, ham, mushrooms, stock and thyme. Cover and cook on LOW for 8–10 hours.

Cut pastry sheets into triangles. Place on an oven tray and bake at 200°C for 10 minutes or until golden. Melt butter and mix in flour. Remove chicken from the slow cooker. Add butter mixture and parsley and mix to combine. Cover and cook on HIGH for 10 minutes.

Remove chicken from bones and mix chicken into the slow cooker. Discard bones. Place chicken mixture in a serving dish. Top with pastry triangles and serve.

Serves 6

chicken with fresh rhubarb relish

2 red onions
3 cloves garlic
4 stalks rhubarb
3 rashers bacon
1 tablespoon curry powder
$^{1}/_{4}$ cup chicken stock
3 tablespoons red wine vinegar
4 skinned and boned chicken breasts
salt and pepper
fresh herbs

Peel onions and cut into thin rings. Crush, peel and finely chop garlic. Trim rhubarb, discarding leaves. Cut stalks into 2cm pieces. Derind bacon and cut into 2cm pieces. Place onions, garlic, rhubarb, bacon, curry powder, chicken stock and vinegar in the slow cooker. Mix to combine. Place chicken breasts on top of rhubarb mixture. Cover and cook on LOW for 8 hours.

Season with salt and pepper. To serve, remove chicken breasts and slice. Spoon rhubarb mixture onto serving plates and top with sliced chicken. Garnish with fresh herbs.

Serves 4–6

chicken à l'orange

2 carrots
1 onion
$\frac{1}{2}$ cup sugar
1 tablespoon grated orange rind
1 cup orange juice
4 skinned and boned chicken breasts
2 tablespoons cornflour
25g soft butter
orange slices

Peel carrots and cut into 1cm cubes. Peel onion and chop finely. Place carrots and onion in the slow cooker. Place sugar in a frying pan and heat slowly until sugar melts and caramelises. Remove from the heat when the sugar is light golden as cooking continues after it is removed from the heat. Carefully stir in orange rind and juice, stirring until combined. Place chicken on top of vegetables and pour sauce over. Cover and cook on LOW for 8 hours.

Mix cornflour and butter together until combined. Stir into sauce in the slow cooker. Turn to HIGH and cook for 10 minutes or until sauce is thick. Serve chicken breasts with sauce, straining if wished to remove vegetables. Garnish with orange slices.

Serves 4–6

slow-cooked christmas turkey

You may have to order the turkey breast ahead of time as these are often in demand at Christmas, thanks to their ease of cooking and carving. This is such an easy way to deal with Christmas cooking and, served with a selection of delicious roast or grilled vegetables and a green salad, what could be more enjoyable! These are great served cold too.

2 skinned and boned turkey breasts
8–10 rashers bacon
$\frac{1}{2}$ cup white wine or chicken stock
2 tablespoons cornflour
3 tablespoons water

STUFFING
1 onion
2 cloves garlic
1 tablespoon lemon olive oil
1 tablespoon balsamic vinegar
1$\frac{1}{2}$ cups fresh breadcrumbs
1 cup grated apple
$\frac{1}{2}$ cup dried cranberries
$\frac{1}{2}$ cup chopped prunes
$\frac{1}{2}$ cup mixed chopped fresh herbs such as parsley, sage and thyme
1 egg
$\frac{1}{2}$ teaspoon salt
$\frac{1}{2}$ teaspoon freshly ground black pepper

Open out the turkey breasts, cutting where necessary so breasts lie flat for stuffing. Divide stuffing between breasts, spreading to within 1cm from the long edge of the breast. Roll breasts up from the long edge. Derind bacon and wrap around breasts. Place in the slow cooker, seam side down. Pour wine or stock over. Cover and cook on HIGH for 2–3 hours, depending on size of breasts.

When ready to serve, mix cornflour and water together. Remove turkey from the slow cooker and cover with foil. Mix cornflour paste into cooking juices. Cover and cook for 10 minutes. Alternatively, strain juices into a saucepan, mix in cornflour paste and cook, stirring until sauce thickens.

Cut turkey into 1cm-thick slices. Pour thickened juices into a gravy boat or jug and serve with sliced turkey.

STUFFING
Peel onion and chop finely. Crush, peel and finely chop garlic. Mix all stuffing ingredients together until combined.

Serves 6–8

meat

Slow cooking deserves a medal for its ability to turn a tough cut of meat into a succulent, tender morsel to be enjoyed in many ways. It enables us to enjoy the important nutrients meat has without needing to take an extra mortgage to pay for it.

sate beef

Rump steak is often on special. That's why I have used it for this recipe. You can use a cheaper cut.

750g beef rump
3 cloves garlic
1 tablespoon medium curry powder
1 tablespoon tamarind pulp
2 tablespoons prepared minced ginger
$1/4$ cup water
bamboo skewers

Trim fat from meat and cut flesh into 2cm cubes. Place in the slow cooker. Crush, peel and finely chop garlic. Mix garlic, curry powder, tamarind pulp, ginger and water together. Pour over meat. Cover and cook on LOW for 8 hours.

Serve threaded on bamboo skewers with steamed rice or naan bread and your favourite dipping sauce. Alternatively, serve unskewered.

Serves 6

spanish beef schnitzel rolls

If you have an aversion to olives, just leave them out. This will still taste great!

6 medium slices beef schnitzel
1 small onion
2 cloves garlic
$1/2$ cup finely chopped pitted green olives
1 cup soft breadcrumbs
2 teaspoons smoked paprika
1 teaspoon ground cumin
1 egg
$1/2$ teaspoon salt
$1/2$ cup beef stock or red wine

Trim any fat from meat and discard. Peel onion and chop finely. Crush, peel and finely chop garlic. Mix onion, garlic, olives, breadcrumbs, paprika, cumin, egg and salt together until combined. Divide stuffing into 6 portions and place a portion along the short edge of each piece of schnitzel. Roll up to enclose stuffing, securing with a toothpick if necessary. Place schnitzel rolls in the slow cooker. Pour stock or wine over. Cover and cook on LOW for 6—8 hours.

Thicken the cooking liquid if wished and serve with rolls.

Serves 6

italian beef stracotto

Stracotto means overcooked, so what better way to cook something that has this requirement than in your very forgiving slow cooker? Porcini mushrooms can be used if you want to make this something special. I would have no hesitation serving it to guests and the porcini mushrooms take it up a notch. This is one dish I would recommend browning before slow cooking.

1.5kg corner cut of topside
2 tablespoons oil
2 onions
3 cloves garlic
2 stalks celery
2 carrots
150g brown button mushrooms
2 bay leaves
1 teaspoon dried sage
1 teaspoon dried thyme
1 cup red wine or beef stock
salt and pepper
fresh herbs

Tie meat to secure if necessary. Heat oil in a large saucepan and brown the meat on all sides. Place in the slow cooker. Peel onions and chop finely. Crush, peel and finely chop garlic. Trim celery and cut into 1cm pieces. Peel carrots and cut into 1cm cubes. Wipe mushrooms and slice. Place onions, garlic, celery, carrots and mushrooms in the slow cooker. Mix bay leaves, sage, thyme and wine or stock together. Pour over meat. Cover and cook on LOW for 10 hours.

Season with salt and pepper. Serve sliced with cooking liquid and vegetables spooned over. Garnish with fresh herbs.

Serves 6

tip

The porcini mushrooms that can be added to this recipe to make it even tastier can be bought dried at gourmet food stores or, in some areas, you may find them at the supermarket.

whole spice
sumatran beef curry

750g chuck, blade or topside steak
2 onions
3 cloves garlic
440g can coconut milk
salt and pepper
lime wedges

CURRY SPICES

1 tablespoon cumin seeds
1 tablespoon black peppercorns
2 tablespoons coriander seeds
2 small dried chillies
4cm piece root ginger
1 stalk lemon grass
3 star anise
6 whole cloves
1 cinnamon quill

Trim fat from meat and discard. Cut meat into 2cm-wide strips. Peel onions and chop finely. Crush, peel and finely chop garlic. Place meat, onion, garlic and coconut milk in the slow cooker. Add spice bag and press into mixture until covered. Cover and cook on LOW for 8–10 hours, mixing halfway through cooking if possible.
   Season with salt and pepper. Serve with lime wedges.

CURRY SPICES
Tie spices in a piece of muslin or clean cloth.

Serves 6

beef and beer pie

This is the sort of dish where you can cook the filling one day, chill it overnight and make a pie the next day. Alternatively, serve the mixture as a casserole rather than a pie. If the meat mixture is used to make a pie while hot, the pastry will become soggy and unappetising.

1kg skirt steak or topside
2 onions
1 carrot
3 rashers bacon
2 teaspoons dried thyme
2 bay leaves
1 teaspoon beef stock powder
3 tablespoons Worcestershire sauce
330ml bottle stout or dark beer
1/2 cup flour
1/2 cup water
400g packet flaky pastry

Trim fat from meat and discard. Cut meat into 2cm chunks. Peel onion and chop finely. Peel carrot and cut into 1cm cubes. Derind bacon and chop into 1cm pieces. Place meat, onion, carrot, bacon, thyme, bay leaves, beef stock powder, Worcestershire sauce and beer in the slow cooker. Mix to combine. Cover and cook on LOW for 8 hours.

Mix flour and water together until smooth and mix into meat. Turn the slow cooker to HIGH and cook for 15 minutes. Remove mixture from the slow cooker and cool.

Cut pastry in half. Roll out one half and use to line the base of a 20cm pie dish. Cut trimmings into a 1cm wide strip. Wet top edge of pastry shell and place pastry strip on top. Fill shell with cold meat mixture. Place a pie funnel in centre of meat if you have one. This stops the centre of the pastry getting soggy and helps the pie brown evenly. Roll remaining pastry for top of pie. Wet edge of pastry shell and place lid on, pressing lightly to seal. Brush pastry top with egg wash. Bake in oven at 200°C for 20–25 minutes or until pastry is golden and cooked.

EGG WASH
1 egg yolk
1 tablespoon water

EGG WASH
Mix egg yolk and water together.

Serves 4–6

tip

Skirt steak is not always available but if you can buy it, do as it gives a much richer coloured and flavoured gravy than other cuts of beef.

kerry ann's fav slow-cooked lamb shanks

These lamb shanks are a favourite recipe of Kerry Ann Dawson who helped in the kitchen for this book. She finds it a great relief to cook something the whole family enjoys and this is one of those dishes.

$^1/_4$ cup flour
1 tablespoon mixed herbs
4–5 lamb shanks
1 onion
3 cloves garlic
2 carrots
2 stalks celery
2 medium potatoes or kumara or a mix of both
$^3/_4$ cup port
$^1/_4$ cup tomato paste
1 cup beef stock
2 tablespoons fresh rosemary leaves
1 tablespoon brown sugar

Mix flour and mixed herbs together. Toss shanks in this and place in the slow cooker. Peel onion and chop finely. Crush, peel and roughly chop garlic. Peel and roughly chop carrots. Trim celery and cut into 1cm slices. Peel and roughly chop potatoes or kumara. Place vegetables in the slow cooker with port, tomato paste, stock, rosemary and brown sugar. Cover and cook on HIGH for 5–6 hours.

Serves 4

tip

If you don't have port on hand, substitute red wine or stock.

lamb shanks with prunes and apples

I sometimes think we become a bit boring using the same old favourite recipes for lamb shanks every time. Add this delicious way to cook lamb shanks to your repertoire when you want to try something different. This dish is wonderful flamed with brandy. Make sure your slow cooker bowl can cope with such high temperatures or do the flaming in another heatproof dish.

1½ cups pitted prunes
¼ cup cider vinegar
350g packet apple slices
¼ cup beef stock
1 onion
2 cloves garlic
2 bay leaves
large sprig fresh thyme
1 good-tasting lemon
4 lamb shanks
salt and pepper
fresh mint

Place prunes in the slow cooker. Mix in vinegar, apple slices and beef stock. Peel onion and chop finely. Crush, peel and finely chop garlic. Mix into apple mixture with bay leaves and thyme. Thinly pare a strip of lemon rind about 6cm long from the lemon. Squeeze juice from lemon and add to the slow cooker with rind. Add lamb shanks to the slow cooker. Cover and cook on LOW for 8–10 hours, turning shanks halfway through cooking if possible. Season with salt and pepper. Serve garnished with mint.

Serves 4

tip

Prunes are so good to cook with as they add flavour and succulence to any dish. Flavoured prunes, or dried plums as they are labelled – probably to overcome resistance some people have to prunes – can be used for a different flavour angle on this dish.

moroccan honey spiced lamb

For a variation in flavour for this recipe, use orange juice instead of water.

1kg boned lamb shoulder
$^1/_2$ cup honey
1 cup raisins
$^1/_2$ cup water
1 teaspoon ground allspice
1 teaspoon ground nutmeg
1 teaspoon ground cinnamon
1 teaspoon ground cardamom
2 teaspoons ground ginger
salt and pepper
toasted, slivered almonds

Trim any fat from meat and discard. Cut meat into large chunks. Place in the slow cooker with honey, raisins, water, allspice, nutmeg, cinnamon, cardamom and ginger. Mix to combine. Cover and cook on LOW for 8 hours. Season with salt and pepper. Serve garnished with toasted almonds.

Serves 6

tip

Always taste food cooked in the slow cooker before serving. Salt and pepper may be needed, and sometimes more spice may be required as some spices lose their intensity when cooked for long periods.

lesley's moving target lamb shanks

I decided it would be great to have a chapter of people's favourite slow cooker recipes in this book but somehow people became coy when asked to give me their recipe. Those who did are featured in the relevant chapters. My cousin Lesley Avery calls this a 'moving target' because it uses whatever needs to be used up in her fridge, so no two brews of this recipe are the same. This is her basic recipe.

1 large onion
1 tablespoon oil
4–6 lamb shanks
2 carrots
2–3 stalks celery
400g can chopped tomatoes
1/4 cup pitted prunes
1/4 cup dried apricots
1 teaspoon Thai green curry paste
1 tablespoon honey
1/2 cup beef stock
salt
parsley

Peel onion and chop. Heat oil in a frying pan and brown onions and shanks. Place in the slow cooker. Peel carrots and cut into cubes. Wash and trim celery. Cut into 1cm slices. Add carrots, celery, tomatoes, prunes, apricots, curry paste and honey to the slow cooker. Add stock to frying pan and heat, scraping pan to remove onions and cooking juices. Pour over shanks in the slow cooker. Cover and cook on HIGH for 2 hours then on LOW for a further 3 hours, or alternatively cook on LOW for 8–10 hours.

Season with salt. Garnish with parsley. Serve with crusty bread to soak up the juices.

Serves 4–6

tip

When creating your own recipe, be wary of combining too many flavours. Sometimes too many different ingredients with different flavours will just end up being lost in your brew, making it a waste of the ingredients.

budget lamb shoulder chops with spiked tomatoes

1 cup orange lentils
2 onions
2 cloves garlic
1 teaspoon ground turmeric
2 teaspoons ground ginger
440g can chopped tomatoes in juice
2 branches parsley
8 lamb shoulder chops
2 tablespoons chopped fresh coriander
lemon wedges

Wash lentils and drain. Place in the slow cooker. Peel onions and chop finely. Crush, peel and finely chop garlic. Add to lentils with turmeric, ginger and tomatoes. Place parsley on top of this mixture. Cut lamb from bones and place in the slow cooker. Mix to combine. Cover and cook on LOW for 8 hours.

Serve garnished with chopped fresh coriander and accompanied by lemon wedges.

Serves 4—6

chinese pork

Use Chinese or Savoy cabbage as an alternative to regular cabbage.

2 medium pork fillets
3 tablespoons fish sauce
2 tablespoons soy sauce
1 teaspoon brown sugar
2 tablespoons white vinegar
1 teaspoon Chinese five spice powder
4 large handfuls finely sliced cabbage
spring onion greens

Trim pork if necessary to remove and fat and sinew. Place in the slow cooker. Mix fish and soy sauces, sugar, vinegar and five spice powder together. Pour over pork. Cover and cook on LOW for 6 hours.

Fifteen minutes before serving, turn the slow cooker to HIGH and place cabbage on top of pork. Cover and cook for 15 minutes. To serve, place cabbage on serving plates. Slice pork and arrange on cabbage. Garnish with spring onion greens.

Serves 4–6

wild pork cooked long and slow

The slow cooker is a great way to cook wild meat and now that wild meat is available to buy for the non-hunters among us, we can all enjoy this great taste experience for a special occasion. Strain and thicken the cooking juices to serve as a sauce with the meat if wished.

2kg boned wild pork
20 red peppercorns
15 juniper berries
2 bay leaves
4 rashers streaky bacon
16 small pickling-sized onions
1 cup black olives
1 cup red wine
1/4 cup balsamic vinegar
bouquet garni of fresh parsley, thyme, celery leaves and bay leaf
salt and freshly ground black pepper

Cut pork into 2cm cubes. Place in the slow cooker with peppercorns, juniper berries and bay leaves. Derind bacon. Cut rashers in half crosswise and roll up from the short side. Add to the slow cooker. Peel onions and add to the slow cooker with olives, wine, vinegar and bouquet garni made by tying the herbs together. Cover and cook on LOW for 10 hours.

Season with salt and pepper. Serve with pasta or a garlic potato mash.

Serves 8

tip

If you enjoy the gamey flavour of wild meat, rest assured slow cooking does not detract from this. It is great for enabling you to serve tender wild meats and you can always turn the slow cooker on in another room such as the laundry so you are not overwhelmed by the cooking smell.

sicilian pork ragù

Replace water with red wine for extra flavour if wished.

1 onion
2 cloves garlic
1 cup drained sundried tomatoes in oil
$\frac{1}{4}$ cup tomato paste
1 cup water
1 sprig rosemary
1 teaspoon dried sage
2 bay leaves
1 pork or bacon hock
500g lean pork pieces
500g pork sausages
fresh herbs

Peel onion and chop finely. Crush, peel and finely chop garlic. Purée sundried tomatoes in a blender or food processor or chop very finely. Mix with tomato paste, water, rosemary, sage, bay leaves, onion and garlic. Remove rind from pork or bacon hock and discard. Place hock, pork pieces and sausages in the slow cooker with sausages on the top layer. Pour tomato mixture over. Cover and cook on LOW for 10 hours.
  Serve with pasta and garnish with fresh herbs.

Serves 6

pork rillette

I first ate pork rillette in France more than 30 years ago and it was such a taste sensation, I still remember how good the experience was. The slow cooker seems perfect for cooking such good-tasting food. Serve this for a summer lunch or on crostini as finger food.

1kg piece pork belly
2 cloves garlic
½ cup white wine
2 sprigs thyme
1 bay leaf
1 cinnamon quill
salt
crusty bread
gherkins

Leave fat on pork. Crush, peel and finely chop garlic. Place wine, garlic, thyme, bay leaf and cinnamon in the slow cooker. Place pork in the slow cooker. Cover and cook on LOW for 10 hours.

Remove pork from the slow cooker. Using 2 forks, shred the meat. Place in a serving dish. If you prefer a smoother rillette, place pork in a food processor and pulse until pork is coarsely shredded. Strain cooking juices through a sieve, season with salt and pour over pork. Cool, then refrigerate until the cooking juices have set.

Serve with crusty bread and gherkins.

Makes about 5 cups

tip

The terrines, pâtés and rillettes we all enjoy when we travel to countries such as France and Italy cook very well in the slow cooker without all the fuss of water baths or bain maries. Pork has become reasonably inexpensive these days so makes a great meat to start with when preparing food for relaxed summer eating.

succulent pork shoulder with crackling

1.3kg boned pork shoulder
1 teaspoon sesame oil
salt
1 tablespoon grated root ginger
2 tablespoons soy sauce
2 tablespoons golden syrup
1 tablespoon fish sauce
2 tablespoons water
1 apple

Score pork rind. Brush with sesame oil and rub with salt. Mix ginger, soy sauce, golden syrup, fish sauce and water together in the bowl of the slow cooker. Place pork on top of this mixture, rind side up. Cover and cook on HIGH for 8 hours.

Carefully remove pork from the slow cooker and place in an ovenproof dish. Core apple and cut into 6 slices. Place in pan with pork. Grill until pork skin is crisp and golden, turning apples during cooking to coat in pan juices. Serve meat sliced with crackling.

Serves 6

pineapple glazed ham hock

This has to be one of the cheapest meals to cook in the slow cooker. A large ham hock will feed 3–4 people and, depending on where you live, can cost as little as $3. If the ham hock looks too big for your slow cooker, ask the butcher to saw off the bottom piece of bone for you.

1 meaty ham hock
432g can pineapple pieces in juice
¼ cup honey
1 tablespoon wholegrain mustard
4 whole cloves
¼ cup dried cranberries
fresh herbs

Remove rind from hock and discard. Place undrained pineapple pieces in the slow cooker. Mix in honey, mustard, cloves and dried cranberries. Add ham hock to the slow cooker. Cover and cook on HIGH for 4 hours.

Cut ham from bone to serve with pineapple and juices spooned over. Garnish with fresh herbs.

Serves 3—4

tip

Boiling bacon or pickled pork make good substitutes for the ham hock used in this recipe. The flavours of the other ingredients will be just as good with these meat cuts and the cooking time will be the same.

venison with beetroot and bacon

1 medium beetroot
1 onion
4 cloves garlic
750g venison
4 rashers bacon
1/4 cup balsamic vinegar
1/4 cup orange juice
3 sprigs thyme
2 tablespoons cornflour
3 tablespoons water
chopped parsley

Peel beetroot and cut into small wedges. Peel onion and chop finely. Crush, peel and finely chop garlic. Cut venison into 2cm cubes. Derind bacon and cut each rasher into quarters. Place beetroot, onion, garlic, venison, bacon, balsamic vinegar, orange juice and thyme in the slow cooker. Mix to combine. Cover and cook on LOW for 6—8 hours.

Mix cornflour and water together and stir into venison mixture. Turn the slow cooker to HIGH and cook for a further 15 minutes. Serve garnished with chopped parsley.

Serves 4—6

tip

Venison is described as low-fat and nutrient-dense meat. Its low fat content makes it more challenging to cook without making it tough but this is not a problem in the slow cooker. Use a tough cut of venison for this recipe. The cost of tender cuts is wasted on slow cooking.

peigi's marsala kidneys

There is nothing that will convince me that kidneys are a joy to eat. I still maintain that the smell of them cooking is like being stuck behind a cattle truck on a long winding stretch of highway. For those who love the flavour of awful offal, this is for you! These are named for Peigi Martin who introduced me to marsala as a secret ingredient for making a casserole taste wonderful.

3 pork kidneys
3 tablespoons flour
1 tablespoon beef stock powder
2 onions
2 cloves garlic
1/4 cup drained capers
1/4 cup marsala
1 teaspoon dried sage
1/4 cup water
salt and pepper
toasted ciabatta or other bread
chopped parsley

Remove membrane and fat from kidneys. Chop kidneys into 2cm cubes. Place flour and stock powder in a plastic bag and toss kidneys in this to coat. Place in the slow cooker. Peel onions and chop finely. Crush, peel and finely chop garlic. Add to kidneys with capers, marsala, sage and water. Cover and cook on LOW for 8 hours.

Season with salt and pepper. Serve on toasted ciabatta, garnished with parsley.

Serves 2–3

tip

The flavour of the other ingredients used in this recipe can be enjoyed by substituting another meat for the kidneys if you prefer.

mince & sausages

Mince and sausages are always great staples to fall back on when you are running low on the housekeeping funds or when you are desperate to find something the whole family will enjoy. Use the recipes that follow as inspiration, based on what you have on hand.

sensational homemade sausages in curry sauce

Choose a ready-made curry sauce flavour that appeals to your palate.

450g sausage meat
250g pork mince
3 tablespoons fish sauce
2 tablespoons lime juice
1 teaspoon prepared minced chilli
1/2 cup finely chopped brown mushrooms
500g jar curry sauce
shredded zucchini
fresh mint

Mix sausage meat, mince, fish sauce, lime juice, chilli and mushrooms together until combined. Take half a cupful at a time and form into sausage shapes. Place in the slow cooker. Pour curry sauce over. Cover and cook on LOW for 6–8 hours.

Serve garnished with shredded zucchini and mint.

Serves 4

sausages in african tomato sauce

8 sausages
400g can savoury tomatoes
1 tablespoon grated root ginger
1/2 teaspoon prepared minced chilli
1/4 cup made up coffee
1/4 cup honey
1 teaspoon ground coriander
1/2 teaspoon ground cumin
fresh herbs

Place sausages in the slow cooker. Mix tomatoes, ginger, chilli, coffee, honey, coriander and cumin together. Pour over sausages. Cover and cook on LOW for 6–8 hours.

Serve garnished with fresh herbs.

Serves 4–6

italian meatballs in slow-cooked vegetable sauce

500g lean mince
1 cup soft breadcrumbs
1 egg
3 tablespoons grated Parmesan cheese
2 teaspoons dried basil
1/2 teaspoon prepared minced chilli
salt and pepper
fresh basil

Mix mince, breadcrumbs, egg, Parmesan cheese, basil and chilli together until combined. Take 2 tablespoons of mixture at a time and roll into balls. Place vegetable sauce ingredients in the slow cooker. Arrange meatballs on top. Cover and cook on LOW for 6–8 hours.

Season with salt and pepper and stir vegetables to combine. If wished, purée the sauce before serving. Serve garnished with fresh basil.

VEGETABLE SAUCE
3 courgettes
2 carrots
3 tomatoes
2 onions
2 cloves garlic
1 teaspoon dried sage
1 teaspoon dried thyme
1 bay leaf

VEGETABLE SAUCE

Trim courgettes and cut into 1cm slices. Peel carrots and cut into 1cm cubes. Roughly chop tomatoes, removing stem end. Peel onions and chop finely. Crush, peel and finely chop garlic. Mix vegetables, sage, thyme and bay leaf together.

Serves 4

tip

Soft breadcrumbs are made from stale bread. I keep the odd piece of stale bread in the freezer and when I have enough to make dirtying the food processor worthwhile, I make soft breadcrumbs. I keep them in a plastic bag in the freezer to use for stuffings, toppings and as a filler for meat loaves and meat balls.

quick-mix moroccan koftas

This is so simple to make and so delicious to eat. Add dried fruit such as raisins or dried apricots and a tablespoon of honey for a tasty variation.

1 onion
500g lean mince
¹/₂ cup soft breadcrumbs
1 egg
1 tablespoon Moroccan spice
440g can Moroccan flavoured tomatoes
2 tablespoons chopped fresh mint
hummus

Peel onion and grate. Place mince in a bowl with breadcrumbs, egg and Moroccan spice. Add onion and mix until well combined. Take 2 tablespoons of mixture at a time and form into torpedo-shaped koftas. Pour tomatoes into the slow cooker and place koftas on top of tomatoes. Cover and cook on LOW for 6—8 hours.

Serve garnished with chopped mint and hummus.

Serves 4—6

rich pasta sauce

500g lean mince
2 carrots
2 onions
3 cloves garlic
2 stalks celery
2 teaspoons dried rosemary
400g can chopped tomatoes
$^{1}/_{4}$ cup tomato paste
$^{1}/_{2}$ cup full-bodied red wine such as shiraz or cabernet sauvignon
$^{1}/_{2}$ teaspoon prepared minced chilli
2 bay leaves
Parmesan cheese shavings

Place mince in the slow cooker, breaking up with a fork to separate meat. Peel carrots and cut into 1cm cubes. Peel onions and chop finely. Crush, peel and finely chop garlic. Trim celery and cut into 1cm cubes. Mix carrots, onions, garlic, celery, rosemary, tomatoes, tomato paste, wine and chilli into mince. Place bay leaves into mixture. Cover and cook on LOW for 6—8 hours.

Serve with cooked pasta topped with shavings of Parmesan cheese.

Serves 4—6

thai chicken sauce with glass noodles

Pork mince can be substituted for chicken mince if preferred.

500g chicken mince
1 onion
2 cloves garlic
1 tablespoon prepared minced ginger
2 teaspoons grated orange rind
$1/4$ cup orange juice
3 tablespoons soy sauce
1 tablespoon white vinegar
165ml can coconut cream
$1/2$ teaspoon ground black pepper
rice vermicelli or pad Thai noodles
chopped fresh coriander or spring onions

Place chicken mince in the slow cooker. Peel onion and chop finely. Crush, peel and finely chop garlic. Mix onion and garlic into mince with ginger, orange rind, juice, soy sauce, vinegar, coconut cream and black pepper. Cover and cook on LOW for 6–8 hours.

Serve with rice vermicelli or pad Thai noodles. Garnish with chopped coriander or spring onions.

Serves 3–4

farmhouse terrine

In my first slow cooker cookbook, Best Recipes for Crockpots & Slow Cookers, I included a recipe for a Pork and Chicken Liver Terrine which is so easy to make, delicious to eat and successfully cooked in the slow cooker that I have enjoyed making this sort of dish regularly when entertaining. Terrines are usually a bit of a fiddle to make and cook but not so with my quick-mix, slow-cooked approach. This one is as fantastic as the one in my first book.

250g chicken livers
4 shallots
2 slices white toast bread
12 black peppercorns
10 whole juniper berries
250g pork sausagemeat
250g chicken mince or boneless, skinless chicken
$\frac{1}{2}$ teaspoon salt
1 tablespoon fresh thyme leaves
2 teaspoons fresh marjoram leaves
$\frac{1}{4}$ cup brandy
10 long rashers streaky bacon
3 bay leaves
crusty bread

Trim sinews and fat from chicken livers and discard. Peel shallots and chop roughly. Tear bread into small pieces. Place chicken livers, shallots, bread, peppercorns, juniper berries, sausagemeat, chicken mince or pieces, salt, thyme, marjoram and brandy in a food processor and process until just combined. Run the back of a knife down the bacon rashers to stretch them. Line the bowl of the slow cooker with bacon so bacon extends up the sides of the bowl. Carefully spread meat mixture into bowl, spreading to edge. Fold bacon over top of meat mixture. Arrange bay leaves on top. Cover and cook on LOW for 6–8 hours.

Carefully run a knife around edge of terrine and turn onto a board. Cool, then wrap in foil and store in fridge until ready to serve. Serve with crusty bread.

Serves 10 as a starter

tip

Run the back of a cook's knife down the length of the bacon rasher to stretch it before using to line the slow-cooker bowl for this terrine, or before using to wrap around chicken or other meat cuts.

vegetarian

Delicious vegetarian food cooked in the slow cooker is a far cry from the mung bean and birdseed idea so many carnivorous people have about vegetarian fare. Even if you are not a vegetarian, try some of these delicious meat-free alternatives for flavour-filled food variety in your life.

three-grain mushroom and spinach risotto with roasted walnuts

1 onion
2 cloves garlic
200g mushrooms
$1/_2$ cup wild rice
1 cup barley
$1/_2$ cup risotto rice
$1/_2$ cup dry white wine
3 cups boiling vegetable stock
2 large handfuls baby spinach
1 cup chopped roasted walnuts
salt and pepper

Peel onion and chop finely. Crush, peel and finely chop garlic. Wipe mushrooms and cut into 0.5cm slices. Place onion and garlic on bottom of the slow cooker and top with mushrooms. Sprinkle wild rice over, then barley then risotto rice. Pour wine and vegetable stock over. Cover and cook on HIGH for 2 hours.

Toss spinach and walnuts through. Season with salt and pepper.

Serves 4–6

puy lentil salad

Don't confine your slow cooker cooking to food to be served hot. Try this as a hot salad if you want, but use your slow cooker to give you a good start for a cold main-course salad.

$1^1/_2$ cups puy lentils
2 cups cold miso soup
2 cloves garlic
2 teaspoons prepared mustard
$1/_4$ cup tarragon vinegar
$1/_2$ cup light olive oil
$1/_4$ teaspoon salt
1 small red onion
4 large handfuls baby salad greens
freshly ground black pepper

Place lentils in the slow cooker. Pour miso soup over. Cover and cook on HIGH for $2^1/_2$–3 hours or until cooked. Drain if necessary. Crush and peel garlic. Place garlic, mustard, vinegar, oil and salt in a screw-top jar. Shake until well combined. Toss through hot lentils. Leave to cool.

Peel onion and cut into thin rings. Mix onion and salad greens together. Toss lentils through. Grind black pepper over and serve. Add herbs with toasted bread if wished.

Serves 6

slow-cooked falafel with tomatoes and tahini dressing

This recipe requires a little forward planning as the chickpeas need to be soaked for 12 hours before they can be ground.

1½ cups dried chickpeas
3 cups parsley leaves
1 onion
6 cloves garlic
1 tablespoon ground cumin
1 tablespoon ground coriander
1 tablespoon baking powder
2 x 400g cans Moroccan flavoured tomatoes

Cover chickpeas with cold water and soak for 12 hours or overnight. Drain and place in a food processor with parsley. Peel onion and chop roughly. Crush and peel garlic. Add onion and garlic to processor and process until mixture is smooth. Add cumin, coriander and baking powder and process until combined. Measure 2 tablespoonsful of mixture at a time and, with wet hands, roll into falafel balls. Pour tomatoes into the slow cooker and add falafel. Cover and cook on LOW for 8 hours.
Serve hot with Tahini Dressing.

TAHINI DRESSING
2 cloves garlic
1 cup natural unsweetened yoghurt
1 tablespoon tahini
3 tablespoons chopped fresh coriander

TAHINI DRESSING
Crush, peel and finely chop garlic. Mix garlic, yoghurt, tahini and coriander together until combined.

Serves 6

tip

Recipes like this using chickpeas or dried beans will soak up the cooking liquid if left to sit for too long after cooking. Add extra water, tomatoes or stock if the mixture becomes too dry before serving. This will certainly apply if leftovers are served the next day.

potato and chickpea curry

If you have access to fresh curry leaves, add 6–8 to the slow cooker for extra flavour.

1 onion
4 cloves garlic
4 medium potatoes
4 tomatoes
1 cup dried chickpeas
$1/4$ cup grated fresh ginger
1 teaspoon cumin seeds
1 teaspoon yellow mustard seeds
1 tablespoon black mustard seeds
1 teaspoon ground turmeric
2 teaspoons ground coriander
3 cups boiling water
$1/2$ teaspoon prepared minced chilli
salt and pepper
chopped parsley for garnish

Peel onion and cut into eighths. Crush, peel and chop garlic. Peel potatoes and cut into 2cm cubes. Cut tomatoes into quarters. Place potatoes, chickpeas, onion, garlic, ginger, tomatoes, cumin, mustard seeds, turmeric and coriander in the slow cooker. Pour boiling water over. Cover and cook on HIGH for 6–8 hours.

Mix in chilli and season with salt and pepper. Serve garnished with parsley.

Serves 4

spicy bean and lentil casserole

Serve this delicious casserole with couscous and drizzled with lemon-infused olive oil if wished.

1 cup fava or haricot beans
1 cup brown lentils
2 onions
2 cloves garlic
6 tomatoes
1 lemon
2 teaspoons ground turmeric
2 teaspoons ground ginger
1 teaspoon cracked black pepper
1½ teaspoons ground cinnamon
2 branches parsley
3 cups boiling water
2 tablespoons chopped fresh
coriander or parsley

Place beans and lentils in the slow cooker. Peel onions and chop finely. Crush, peel and finely chop garlic. Chop tomatoes roughly, removing and discarding stem end. Quarter lemon and add with onions, garlic, tomatoes, turmeric, ginger, pepper, cinnamon and parsley to the slow cooker. Pour boiling water over. Cover and cook on HIGH for 8–10 hours.

Remove parsley branches and serve sprinkled with chopped fresh coriander or parsley.

Serves 6

pumpkin, bean and rice casserole

This is a great dish to make when you have some leftover cooked rice. It is delicious served with a tamarind chutney.

1½ cups aduki beans
400g peeled and deseeded pumpkin
2 onions
4 cloves garlic
4cm piece root ginger
2 tablespoons red curry paste
2 teaspoons ground cardamom
1 teaspoon ground turmeric
3 cups boiling vegetable stock
2 cups cooked rice
1 teaspoon garam masala
¼ cup chopped fresh mint
½ teaspoon prepared minced chilli
¼ cup lemon juice
fresh mint

Place beans in the slow cooker. Cut pumpkin into 2cm pieces. Peel onions and chop finely. Crush, peel and finely chop garlic. Grate root ginger. Place pumpkin on top of beans. Sprinkle onion and garlic over. Mix curry paste, ginger, cardamom, turmeric and vegetable stock together. Pour over ingredients in the slow cooker. Cover and cook on HIGH for 8 hours.

An hour before dish is ready to serve, mix rice, garam masala, chopped mint and chilli together and place on top of ingredients in the slow cooker. Cover and cook for an hour. When ready to serve, mix lemon juice through. Serve garnished with mint.

Serves 4–6

desserts

I am still in awe of how well the slow cooker cooks desserts! The way it performs when cooking these desserts makes me wonder if some cooks could manage to do without a conventional oven. Try some of these recipes and you will see what I mean.

poached berries with meringue islands

500g frozen mixed red berries
2 tablespoons sugar
2 tablespoons cornflour
2 egg whites
$^1/_2$ cup sugar
1 teaspoon icing sugar
$^1/_2$ teaspoon cinnamon

Place berries in the slow cooker. Mix first measure of sugar and cornflour together and mix through berries. Beat egg whites until peaks form. Beat in second measure of sugar until mixture is thick and glossy. Using 2 dessert spoons, form meringue mixture into egg shapes and place on top of berries. Cover and cook on LOW for 2 hours.

Mix icing sugar and cinnamon together. Serve warm or cold, dusted with icing sugar mixture.

Serves 4

lemon tart

1 sheet sweet short pastry
25g butter
$^1/_2$ cup sugar
2 eggs
$^1/_4$ cup lemon juice
1 teaspoon grated lemon rind
$^1/_4$ cup cornflour

Cut a round of baking paper 2.5cm larger than base of the slow cooker. Make 2.5cm cuts from edge of paper on the diagonal. Place paper in the slow cooker. It needs to come above pastry edges to allow tart to be removed from the slow cooker without breaking. Place pastry evenly on baking paper. Cut pastry corners off to make an even edge. Melt butter. Mix in sugar, eggs, lemon juice and rind and cornflour, and mix with a wooden spoon until smooth. Pour into pastry shell. Cover and cook on HIGH for 2 hours.

Use a large fish slice and the paper to carefully remove the tart from the slow cooker.

Serves 4–6

slow-cooked caramel spiced nectarines

When I wrote this recipe, I thought the sweetened condensed milk would caramelise as it cooked. This happened around the edges, but the juice from the fruit probably prevented it from happening all the way through the condensed milk. It was delicious anyway!

400g can sweetened condensed milk

2 star anise

$1/2$ teaspoon dried pink peppercorns

4 large, firm ripe apricots, nectarines or peaches

1 tablespoon melted butter

Mix condensed milk, star anise and pink peppercorns together and place in the slow cooker. Cut fruit in half and remove stones. Brush fruit with melted butter and place on top of condensed milk. Cover and cook on LOW for $2^{1}/_2$ hours.

Serve warm or cold with runny cream if wished.

Serves 4

thai rice pudding

This is delicious served with grilled pineapple rings. To make these, place drained canned or fresh pineapple rings under the grill, in a hot cast iron pan or on a barbecue and cook until golden. Drizzle with extra coconut cream to serve if wished

1 cup arborio rice	Place rice, sugar, coconut cream, coconut, lime cordial and crushed kaffir lime leaf in the slow cooker. Mix to combine. Cover and cook on LOW for 4 hours.
1/4 cup sugar	
2 cups coconut cream	
1/2 cup shredded coconut	Serve hot garnished with fresh lime slices. If left to serve cold, the pudding will thicken so mix in extra coconut cream to give the preferred consistency.
1/4 cup lime cordial	
1 kaffir lime leaf	
fresh lime slices	Serves 4—6

cranberry and orange christmas pudding

Working for 22 years as a magazine food editor always provided a challenge for me to come up with new ideas for Christmas fare. Cranberries are an obvious choice for a Christmas pudding, yet I have never written a recipe for one, so here is a slow-cooked option.

6 slices stale wholemeal toast bread
1 cup orange juice
1½ cups raisins
2½ cups dried cranberries
½ cup sugar
2 tablespoons cornflour
2 teaspoons mixed spice
1 teaspoon cinnamon
125g butter
1 teaspoon vanilla essence
1 teaspoon natural orange or lemon essence
3 eggs
1 oven bag

Leave crusts on bread and cut slices into 1.5cm cubes. Place in a mixing bowl and pour in orange juice. Mix with a knife to break up bread. Mix in raisins, cranberries, sugar, cornflour, mixed spice and cinnamon. Melt butter and add to bread with vanilla and orange essences. Separate eggs and mix yolks into mixture. Beat egg whites until stiff and fold into fruit mixture. Cut sealed end from oven bag and secure with string or a heat-proof tie. Spoon mixture into oven bag so the secured centre of the bag is in the centre base of the pudding. Secure top of bag and place in slow cooker. Cover and cook on HIGH for 2 hours.

Carefully remove from bag. Serve hot with brandy sauce, custard or ice cream.

Serves 6–8

tip

This is a great Christmas pudding to make if you like home-cooked puddings but have not had the time to make one in advance. It is deliciously moist and flavour-filled without the ageing from cooking weeks or months in advance. It is especially good served with lightly whipped cream. For something even more special, try drizzling the cream with pomegranate syrup.

old-fashioned apple dumplings

As a child I was a 'fussy eater' with a great dislike for many of the dishes my poor mother tried to feed me. There is not much I remember from my childhood food experiences other than the things I disliked. Apple dumplings are one memory of delicious food I do have so I have tried to recreate these memorable flavours in this slow-cooked version.

2 cups self-raising flour
100g butter
1/2 cup milk
4 apples
2 tablespoons sugar
1 teaspoon cinnamon
1/2 teaspoon ground cloves

Place flour and butter in a food processor and process until mixture looks like fine crumbs. With motor running pour enough milk down feed tube to make a stiff dough. Alternatively, make the dough by rubbing in butter and mixing in enough milk to make a stiff dough. Roll dough out thinly on a lightly floured board. Cut into squares large enough to enclose the apples. Peel and core apples, leaving whole. Place an apple in the centre of each pastry square. Mix sugar, cinnamon and cloves together and sprinkle over apples. Bring pastry corners together over apples and press edges together to enclose fruit. Place in the slow cooker. Pour syrup over. Cover and cook on HIGH for 2–2 1/2 hours or until apples are cooked. To test if apples are cooked, poke with a skewer.

Serve hot with ice cream.

SYRUP
1 cup sugar
3/4 cup water
2 tablespoons butter
1 teaspoon cinnamon
1 teaspoon ground cloves

SYRUP

Place sugar, water, butter, cinnamon and cloves in a saucepan and bring to the boil, stirring until sugar dissolves.

Serves 4

tip

If you have the opportunity, baste these dumplings with the syrup halfway through cooking. Alternatively, drizzle the syrup over before serving as this will make the dumplings look more appetising.

french pears

I have looked at recipes for pears poached in red wine in books over the years and have never been bothered to make them. They seemed too much of a fiddle to cook to perfection and not flash on great flavour either, so why would you bother? Such desserts do look stunning so I thought the slow cooker would be just the thing for ensuring perfection and a great eating experience. I wasn't wrong!

4 ripe firm pears
2 cups red wine
1 cup sugar
2 cinnamon sticks
1 star anise
1 vanilla bean
3 cardamom pods
2 oranges
whipped cream

Peel pears and place lying down in the slow cooker. Mix wine and sugar together. Pour over pears. Add cinnamon sticks, star anise, vanilla bean and cardamom pods to the slow cooker. Thinly peel rind from one orange and squeeze juice. Add to the slow cooker. Cut remaining orange into 4 thick slices and add to the slow cooker. Cover and cook on HIGH for 2–2¹/₂ hours or until pears are tender.

Turn pears halfway through cooking. Serve warm or cold with softly whipped cream.

Serves 4

index